LINK ACROSS AMERICA

MORE PRAISE FOR LINK ACROSS AMERICA

LINK ACROSS AMERICA

A STORY OF THE HISTORIC LINCOLN HIGHWAY

Mary Elizabeth Anderson

Rayve Productions

Rayve Productions Inc.
Box 726 Windsor CA 95492 USA

Printed in USA

Publisher's Cataloging in Publication
Anderson, Mary Elizabeth
    Link across America: a story of the historic Lincoln Highway /
by Mary Elizabeth Anderson; selected illustrations by Randall F. Ray
p. cm.
    Includes bibliographical references, map, photographs.
    ISBN 1-877810-97-5

    1. Lincoln Highway—History. 2. Automobile travel—
United States—History—Juvenile literature. 3. United States—
Social life and customs—History—Juvenile literature.

I. Ray, Randall F., ill. II. Title
HE356.L7A64 1997   388.1'0973
                        QBI97-40120

Library of Congress Catalog Card Number 97-65052

FRONT COVER: Stretch of brick road west of Omaha,
Nebraska—near Elkhorn, Nebraska—built in 1919.
Photo by author.

Contents

DEDICATION

To my dad, who traveled many miles on the Lincoln Highway during his lifetime and to my husband, Don, who continues to explore the highway with me.

—M.E.A.

ACKNOWLEDGMENTS

This book would not have been possible without the loving support and encouragement of my family, and the helpful assistance of long-time friends Bob and Joyce Ausberger. I also want to thank my publishers, Barbara and Norm Ray, for all their help; various members of the Lincoln Highway Association, who consented to review my manuscript and provided additional information and photographs; and Becky Junker, Merry von Seggern and Dandi Daley Mackall, who willingly gave of their time to serve as reviewers.

—M.E.A.

Road Rally

Children raced out of Seedling Mile School and joined the crowd that gathered on the sidewalk in front of the building. Mrs. McElroy, their teacher, had announced early that morning that a road rally would soon arrive at their school.

Seedling Mile School

©1997 Randall Ray

This road rally had started in another state, and along the way, drivers of antique cars from many towns had joined the procession. All the antique cars in the road rally had been restored by their owners, who enjoyed sharing stories about their work on the cars and the trips they had taken in them.

Mrs. McElroy told the children that important people would speak to the group. She said photographers would take pictures and newspaper reporters would write stories about the old cars and about Seedling Mile School.

Dozens of Classic Cars

The boys and girls watched as several dozen cars pulled into the parking lot. There were many makes and models, and they all had red, white and blue flags hanging from their hoods. All the people in the cars belonged to an organization called the Lincoln Highway Association.

Mrs. McElroy gave the children permission to look more closely at the cars and to speak to the drivers. They first talked with a friendly man who introduced himself as Dan. His car was turquoise and white.

Juan ran his hands up and down the car's silver chrome and asked, "What kind of car is this?"

Dan smiled proudly. "This, kids, is a 1957 Chevy Bel Air. It's a classic style and was very popular when it was new. Do you think you'd like to drive it?"

"Yes," said Ling. "It's cool! I like those big fenders and the way that curved piece gets wider toward the back. I wish my dad had a car like that. Did you fix it up by yourself?"

"Sure did," said Dan. "It took me three years. That's a long time to work on a car, but I really enjoyed it. Now it's in great shape. And, by the way, we call those big fenders 'fins.'"

"Wow! Three years!" said Grant. "Why did it take so long?"

"Well, first I had to take the car apart, then repair the pieces that didn't work so well

anymore. And, when I finished all that, I had to put it back together again. Now this car is worth a lot of money. But, I'm not going to sell it. I'll give it to my son someday."

"I'm going to talk to my dad and see if we can fix up an old car, too," said Juan.

"Hey, look at this one," Sara shouted, as the boys and girls moved toward the next car in line. "This car looks kind of funny, but I like it. What kind do you think it is?"

"It's a Model T Ford," said the driver, stepping out from behind the car. His name, Dean, was boldly printed on his name tag. "It's a great looking car, isn't it? This make was the first really popular car. They used to call it a 'Tin Lizzie.' Some people still do."

"It sort of looks like a stagecoach to me," said Maria. "Or, maybe something like an old buggy."

©1997 Randall Ray

"You're right," said Dean with a smile. "Since it was among the early cars made, it does resemble the old buggies. Some folks referred to them as 'horseless carriages.'"

The children looked at the rest of the cars and talked with the drivers. They especially liked a sleek green car that had a long hood and a short roofline. They asked the driver why the license plate read 64 TBRD. He told them it meant his car was a "1964 Thunderbird."

Seedling Miles and the Lincoln Highway

Do you wonder why these men and women gathered for a road rally? Do you wonder why people considered Seedling Mile School important?

Well, the school was named after a "seedling mile" road that ran nearby. This seedling mile road was one of the first double lane, paved rural mile sections in the state.

Seedling miles were important to people who made the first well-planned roadway across the United States. Because it ran from the east coast to the west coast, they called it a transcontinental (trans-con-ti-nen-tal) highway. They named it the Lincoln Highway.

A Warm Welcome

The president of the chamber of commerce said, "Welcome boys, girls and teachers. And, welcome to Lincoln Highway Association members gathered here. We're happy you stopped at our school."

Many people stood around a sign that said "Seedling Mile School" as they listened to him.

Mr. Boomer, a man from the Lincoln Highway Association, spoke next. He said that after 1925, many parts of the Lincoln Highway were renamed, but in many areas, people still call it the Lincoln Highway. Then, Mr. Boomer told the group some stories about how the roadway began.

Horse and Buggy Days

When the first automobiles were invented, they were not widely used. By 1900 people were beginning to seriously consider automobiles as a method of transportation. But, autos in

America were rare and expensive. Most people could not afford to own a motor vehicle. Instead, they walked, traveled by train, by horse and buggy, or by bicycle.

From 1877 until about 1902 many bicycle clubs were formed. For personal transportation, bicycles were the first step forward from the horse and buggy. Adults, as well as children, loved to ride bicycles. Then, in 1903 the Ford Motor Company began mass producing lower priced motor vehicles, and people started to get excited about owning cars.

However, even if a person owned a car, he or she couldn't drive a great distance. Most of the roads throughout the United States were just plain dirt, and they didn't go very far. Most of them ran only from the farm to town and the train depot. A farmer could easily travel to town with his products, but if he wanted to go into the next town, he usually had to take a train.

"Boxcars, flatcars, tank cars and hoppers rode the train tracks," said Mr. Boomer. "So did rail passenger cars. Trains carried people, food and other supplies clear across the United States. People liked to ride trains, but trains didn't give them the freedom to travel wherever they wanted to go as the new automobiles did."

Follow the Sun

Then Mr. Boomer told them about Carl Fisher, a man who often had great ideas and dreamed about creating a very special highway across America. He had once been a bicycle salesman and racer, and later became a race car driver. He even broke a few world records back then.

Carl Fisher
"Father" of the
Lincoln Highway

W. Earl Givens collection

Carl Fisher had already started the Indianapolis 500 car race and the thought of creating a coast-to-coast highway excited him.

Every day Carl Fisher spoke to anyone who would listen to him about his dream. He wanted to follow the sun as had other pioneers before him. But, he didn't want to ride on horseback or struggle along on the old trails. He wanted to drive a car across America on a well-marked, improved pathway built for motor vehicles.

Henry B. Joy

Henry B. Joy
First President of the
Lincoln Highway
Association

Carl Fisher discussed his dream with a man named Henry B. Joy, the president of the Packard Motor Car Company. He liked the idea, too. And, because Mr. Joy had always admired Abraham Lincoln, the 16th president of the United States, he wanted to dedicate the highway to him.

President Lincoln's Legacy

Mr. Boomer explained that many people admired Abraham Lincoln. They looked up to him, because he was a fair man who wanted all of America's people to be free. On November 19, 1863, President Lincoln gave a famous speech at Gettysburg, Pennsylvania. People never forgot his talk. He wanted people everywhere to understand what freedom means and how much we owe to the brave soldiers who died at Gettysburg. He wanted everyone to remember that all people

have an equal right to life, liberty and the pursuit of happiness. President Lincoln believed that a country could not survive as half slave and half free.

The children liked hearing about Abraham Lincoln. A statue of him stood in front of their county court house, and most of them had walked by it many times. Mrs. McElroy had told them that 38 cities in the United States are named after President Lincoln.

The children had also learned about the huge statue of President Lincoln in the Lincoln Memorial in Washington D.C. It was built to honor President Lincoln, and it reminds Americans of his greatness. The boys and girls felt proud that Abraham Lincoln showed kindness and understanding to everyone. The children were glad people named a highway after him.

Mr. Boomer paused when Maria raised her hand. Maria said, "Our family visited the Lincoln Memorial on vacation last summer. We really liked seeing the statue, and I took some pictures of it."

After Maria finished speaking, Mr. Boomer continued his story about Mr. Fisher's dream for a transcontinental highway that would bind the nation together and be free to anyone who wished to use it.

Mr. Fisher, Mr. Joy and several other leaders agreed that the United States needed the highway. However, they also realized they couldn't plan and build a roadway by themselves. They would need the help of many people to finish the job.

The Lincoln Highway Association

So, in 1913 the men formed a large group called the Lincoln Highway Association. Many people interested in a new highway joined the group. An association works somewhat like a club, and the members held meetings to discuss their plans.

After much discussion and preparation, Lincoln Highway Association members decided the highway should follow the most direct path between both coasts. Some stretches of the new roadway would be built along parts of the transcontinental railroad route, but other road sections would wind through new territory.

Twelve States

The Lincoln Highway Association directors decided the highway should start at Times Square in New York City. The roadway would run southwest through New Jersey, west through Pennsylvania, and then loop through Ohio and Indiana. It would wind its way onto the prairies of Illinois, Iowa and Nebraska. Then the highway would cut through Wyoming, Utah and Nevada, ending at Lincoln Park in San Francisco, California.

Following this route, the highway would run from the Atlantic Ocean clear across the United States to the Pacific Ocean.

Mrs. McElroy's students whispered to one another when they heard the states mentioned. Many of the children had visited one or two of them during summer vacations.

Building Seedling Mile Road Sections

Mr. Boomer told the crowd the highway started as 3,389 miles of mostly dirt trails and gravel roads. Then the Portland Cement Company wrote on behalf of the cement industry and offered to donate three million barrels of cement for the new highway. The Lincoln Highway

Association used this cement to make sections of road across the country. They called these sections "Seedling Miles."

The children's ears perked up when they heard "Seedling Miles." They started to whisper again. Many of them had wondered why their school had such an unusual name.

Mr. Boomer explained that the seedling miles were simply strips of hard-surfaced roadway that were usually only one mile in length. They showed people the work of the Lincoln Highway Association, and they were examples of top quality roads. Motorists from miles around enjoyed driving on the smooth, even road surfaces.

Mr. Boomer said, "There was no government money for roads in those early years. In fact, 20 states had no road departments of any kind. The Lincoln Highway Association had hoped people living along the chosen sections would give money to help build the rest of the road. Many people did."

Children and the Lincoln Highway

Children helped with the Lincoln Highway, too. Some school classes collected

Lincoln pennies, and when they had 500 pennies, they sent them to the Lincoln Highway Association for a membership. Some Boy Scout troops helped set concrete Lincoln Highway marker posts. And, just for fun, many children used to sit beside the Lincoln Highway to see how many out-of-state cars they could spot.

How Wide Should A Road Be?

At first, no one knew how wide to make the road sections. After some discussion, the association decided on ten feet in width. Then the men changed their minds. They settled on sixteen to twenty feet, reasoning that if a horse-drawn hayrack should meet a truck along the way, they would need plenty of room to pass one another.

Illinois and the First Seedling Mile

Mr. Joy wanted to make seedling miles of road in Illinois, Iowa, Nebraska, Wyoming, Utah and Nevada. Folks in Illinois wanted the first seedling mile in their state, so they worked hard to

ILLINOIS

raise money. With the promise of free cement from the Lincoln Highway Association, supporters raised the $2,000 they needed to begin work. The state then had the land surveyed and offered road building equipment and engineering supervision.

Then, a group called the Good-Roads People, of DeKalb, Illinois, got their resources together and asked the Lincoln Highway Association for cement. The secretary of the association said, "The ball is opened and you are the leader of the first dance." This meant that the folks in Illinois would get the first 2,000 barrels of cement, and Illinois proudly claimed the first mile. Workers finished it in 1914.

Hard Work

Building the highway was not easy. Most of the roads were just plain dirt. Before the

new roads were paved, when it rained or snowed, the mud would often get so deep no one could drive through it.

Also, few counties had big, powerful road building equipment as they do today. Most road work was done with hand-held picks and

shovels and horse-drawn teams pulling scrapers and graders. It was very hard work.

The children stared at the street in front of their school in amazement. It was hard to imagine a team of horses working there.

One elderly man from the road rally spoke out, "My cousin once lived in the next county. But, after workers finished the seedling mile here, he decided to attend school in this county. He wanted to change schools because he owned a car and he liked to drive on the new concrete road. The strips of paved roadway created lots of excitement when I was a young man."

Mr. Boomer said seedling miles were among the first improvements the Lincoln Highway Association planned. In 1913 they announced the route, and in 1914 they began graveling and grading the roadways. In 1915 workers made four seedling miles. It took the crews many years to finish the highway.

New Numbers for Roads

The highway had the Lincoln name for a short period of time. Then, in 1926 the government decided to mark all United States roads by numbers. It did this so people could recognize roads more easily. The government gave east/west roads even numbers and north/south roads odd numbers. In the eastern part of the United States, the Lincoln Highway was renamed Highway 1. From eastern Pennsylvania to near Salt Lake City, Utah, it became U.S. 30. And, in the West, it is known as U.S. 40 and U.S. 50. Throughout much of the United States today, I-80 closely follows the original Lincoln Highway.

How the Lincoln Highway Helped People

"The Lincoln Highway accomplished much in its brief, active life," said Mr. Boomer. "Because of it, factories sprang up across the country. The factories made products like clothing, automobile parts, appliances and hardware. These factories created jobs for many people. New trucks were designed to transport goods on the highway. Trucks carried products made in the factories, and made it easier and faster to get factory goods from the east coast to the west coast."

 The Lincoln Highway became a model for many roads that followed, because it served as America's first coast-to-coast thoroughfare. The people who later developed interstates learned from the experiences of those who had built roads before them.

The children listened closely to the speech. They enjoyed hearing Mr. Boomer talk about the highway, Abraham Lincoln, and the seedling miles.

Making Concrete

The following day, Mrs. McElroy asked, "Do any of you know how to make concrete? Have you watched men make new streets around town? Concrete is made by mixing sand, gravel, cement and water together in a barrel. When the barrel turns, it blends the ingredients thoroughly until the mixture is ready to pour. When the mixture hardens, it turns to concrete."

Abbie raised her hand and said, "My dad made concrete for the new step in front of our house. It was hard work, but he did a good job. It really looks nice."

The New Lincoln Highway Association

Mrs. McElroy told the class that a new national Lincoln Highway Association had recently been formed in Iowa. She said the new group's members plan to preserve the memory of this historic route—

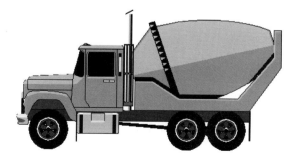

America's first transcontinental highway. They also want to save the remaining road markers, monuments, and historic buildings along the roadway.

Burma-Shave Signs

The class learned that a shaving cream company, the Burma-Vita Company, used to place funny signs along the highway.

Burma-Shave

SHAVERS GROW

LET THE LITTLE

TAKE IT SLOW

SCHOOLHOUSES

PAST

Mrs. McElroy said, "I bet some of your grandparents remember Burma-Shave signs. Why don't you ask them? And, tell them the new Lincoln Highway Association wants to put some of the funny signs back up."

For 36 years, beginning in 1927, Burma-Shave signs were placed along the nation's roads. Back then, the electric razor had not been invented so men had to shave with straight razors or safety razors. Shaving cream made shaving with the old-style razors easier.

Motorists thought Burma Shave jingles were funny, and the signs were good advertising for the Burma-Vita Company. So, the company put up hundreds of signs along the nation's roads.

The children decided to locate as many Burma-Shave jingles as possible. Mrs. McElroy asked them to share their jingles at school the following week.

It surprised Mrs. McElroy that so many of the children's grandparents remembered the signs. Sara said her grandma's favorite was:

EVERY SHAVER • NOW CAN SNORE • SIX MORE MINUTES • THAN BEFORE • BY USING • Burma-Shave

Juan said his grandpa liked:

| GOLFERS! | IF FEWER STROKES | ARE WHAT YOU CRAVE | YOU'RE OUT OF THE ROUGH | WITH | *Burma-Shave* |

The boys and girls laughed when they read their jingles.

"How many of you would like to make a booklet of the Burma-Shave jingles?" Mrs. McElroy asked.

Every hand flew up.

"Wonderful!" she said. "Just continue to collect as many Burma-Shave jingles as possible, and we'll put them into a nice booklet for our school library."

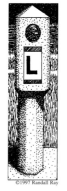

Historic Old Highway Markers

The class then visited a park located in the center of town. Mrs. McElroy pointed out that the Lincoln Highway, or Highway 30, runs right by the park. She took the children to a special section, and asked them how many had noticed the large Lincoln Highway sign, which town leaders had put in the park many years ago. Mrs. McElroy pointed out two Lincoln Highway markers beside the sign. She said only about twelve markers still exist in their original locations. The children could see faint red, white and blue stripes still on the two markers in the park.

The children noticed that the Highway 30 sign was old and cracked. Narrow marks ran over it like fine lines in a cobweb, and it was painted black and white—just like modern Highway 30 signs.

Some of the children brought cameras so they could take pictures of this special section of the park. They liked the way people saved the memory of the Lincoln Highway so everyone could learn about it.

Grant raised his hand and said, "My dad talked to the president of the new Lincoln Highway Association at a meeting. The president said she hopes tour groups will visit sections of the Lincoln Highway. She thinks writers, artists and other people will enjoy seeing it, too. She said the association now has its headquarters in Franklin Grove, Illinois. They intend to build a museum there. The museum will have all sorts of good stuff in it."

Bricks and Bridges

"My dad and I drove on the brick road section of the Lincoln Highway near Elkhorn, Nebraska," Mark said. "It was almost a mile long, and Dad and I liked the bumpy way it felt

©1997 Randall Ray

when we went over the bricks."

"My family might take a trip to see the bridge in Tama, Iowa," Abbie said. "Mom wants to see the Lincoln Highway name on the guardrails. My grandpa said men made the name out of forms that molded the concrete."

Mrs. McElroy told the class more history of the old highway. The boys and girls liked hearing about it. She passed around photographs of some of the original gas stations and cabin courts along the road. She said some people enjoy visiting these places, and some like to hunt for monuments and statues along the highway.

"Do any of your parents like antiques?" Mrs. McElroy asked.

Many of the boys and girls raised their hands.

"Many people interested in antiques have joined the Lincoln Highway Association," she said. "They enjoy things like old cars, trucks and bicycles. Some of these people like to collect old postcards or other objects, too. And, they like to discover old soda fountains, diners, cabin courts, gas stations and

bridges. Why don't you boys and girls look for good pictures of these items, and we'll make a scrapbook with them, too," she said.

The Modern Lincoln Highway

The class had learned many interesting things about the old Lincoln Highway.

"Now let's see if we can find the Lincoln Highway on these maps," Mrs. McElroy said.

She unfolded several large maps, and the children gathered around to look at them. Mrs. McElroy pointed out on the map where interstate highways have replaced many smaller two-lane highways.

She said, "Interstate highways have existed for more than 40 years, and some drivers like to hurry down these straight roadways. But many people think interstates make travel less interesting because they usually don't wind through towns."

Mrs. McElroy said, "Look, boys and girls. See where Interstate 80 runs?"

The children nodded.

"See how Interstate 80 goes straight across the country? It may be the best way to travel if you're in a hurry.
But, now look at these old winding roads. Which way do you think would be the most fun to travel?"

The children all responded by saying, "The old roads!"

Saving the Old Lincoln Highway

Many people are interested in saving the history of the Lincoln Highway. It helps to tell the story of transportation. The road remains part of a time many remember. Much of our country came together and grew along the highway. Now, many people want to look back at the way we've traveled. And, they want to share their special memories with boys and girls like you.

Many folks want to remember the mud roads that connected towns and villages. They want to remember how old roads were turned into brick and concrete pavement. These roads brought many Americans together.

Those people helping to save the Lincoln Highway like the slower pace of life. When they drive down the road, they appreciate a good view of towns, fields, and crops along the way. They enjoy a close look at the beauty of nature and the changing seasons.

Many people still like to drive down highways that go through main streets of towns, to see the older buildings and homes located there. Passengers like to wave to children riding their bicycles. It's also fun for motorists to stop and visit in gas stations and restaurants.

Most of all, many people like to remember the Lincoln Highway and everyone who lived along it. These folks enjoy preserving memories. They also like to think about our great 16th president, Abraham Lincoln, and the brave way he helped stop slavery in our country.

We should not forget this exciting story of transportation. We should remember how hard others worked to develop the first transcontinental roadway that became the link across America. The great Lincoln Highway made it possible to travel by car clear across the United States.

MORE BURMA-SHAVE JINGLES

EENY-MEENY
MINY-MO
SAVE YOUR SKIN
YOUR TIME
YOUR DOUGH
BURMA SHAVE

HIS TENOR VOICE
SHE THOUGHT DIVINE
TILL WHISKERS
SCRATCHED
SWEET ADELINE
BURMA SHAVE

NO LADY LIKES
TO DANCE
OR DINE
ACCOMPANIED BY
A PORCUPINE
BURMA-SHAVE

EVERY DAY
WE DO
OUR PART
TO MAKE YOUR FACE
A WORK OF ART
BURMA-SHAVE

THE BEARDED LADY
TRIED A JAR
SHE'S NOW
A FAMOUS
MOVIE STAR
BURMA-SHAVE

THIS IS NOT
A CLEVER VERSE
I TRIED
AND TRIED
BUT JUST GOT WORSE
BURMA-SHAVE

THO LIVING COSTS
ARE UPWARD BOUND
FOUR BITS
STILL BUYS
HALF A POUND
BURMA-SHAVE

BRISTLY BEARD
OR SILKY FUZZ
JUST SHAVE 'EM BACK
TO WHERE
THEY WAS
BURMA-SHAVE

AT CROSSROADS
DON'T JUST
TRUST TO LUCK
THE OTHER CAR
MAY BE A TRUCK
BURMA-SHAVE

Author's note: Seedling Mile School (page 7) and the park the children visited (pages 26 and 27, Pioneer Park) are located in Grand Island, Nebraska. The statue of Abraham Lincoln at the county courthouse (page 15) is located in Jefferson, Iowa.

THE LINCOLN HIGHWAY YESTERDAY AND TODAY

These markers designate the first section of the Lincoln Highway named to the National Register of Historic Places. The section of road is west of Omaha, near Elkhorn, Nebraska.

This brick section of the Lincoln Highway was built in 1919.

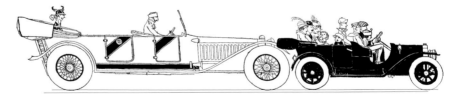

Except where indicated otherwise, photos are from the author's collection.

The Lincoln Highway was dedicated to the memory of President Abraham Lincoln. The statue shown above stands in front of Greene County courthouse in Jefferson, Iowa.

A number of Lincoln Highway monuments were built as memorials to men who helped with highway improvement. This monument honors J. E. Moss of Scranton, Iowa.

The Lincoln Highway Bridge at Tama, Iowa is well known. Each letter was molded out of concrete.

An American flag proudly waves from the front porch of this neat farmhouse on the Lincoln Highway near Scranton, Iowa.

This gas station was a busy place after George Preston opened it in 1923 in Belle Plaine, Iowa. Today, people still like to stop by to look at the many old signs.

This monument in Wyoming (Exit 184, I-80) honors Henry Joy, the first president of the Lincoln Highway Association.

Orr's Ranch was once a welcome sight to drivers on the Lincoln Highway in Utah. In 1916 a tired traveler could rest and enjoy a hot meal here. Many people still enjoy visiting the old log building today.

Concrete bridges like this one in Boone County, Iowa were important early Lincoln Highway improvements.

Eureka Bridge gracefully spans the Raccoon River west of Jefferson, Iowa.

An original part of the Lincoln Highway in Greene County, Iowa. Like many old roads, this one is not paved.

Donner Pass Bridge, sometimes called a "rainbow bridge," is located on the old Lincoln Highway in California's Sierra Nevada mountains.

Bob Ausberger collection

An old farm tractor rests beside the Lincoln Highway.

University of Michigan Library collection

Henry B. Joy, first president of the original Lincoln Highway Association, drove his Packard Twin Six through Iowa mud in 1915. Mr. Joy put the hood up to help cool the car's engine.

B.J.F. Ray collection

Before roads were improved, most travelers driving long distances camped beside the road at the end of the day. There were few hotels and restaurants along the old roadways.

William Schneider, Sr. collection

The Model T Ford could go 40 miles per hour and run 22 miles on a gallon of gasoline. Over 15,000,000 were sold between 1912 and 1927.

B.J.F. Ray collection

Trucks carried factory products from the east coast to the west coast on the Lincoln Highway.

The first concrete highway in Indiana was built in Allen County in 1914. The Brooks Construction Company of Ft. Wayne, Indiana did the work with the help of many men and a Koehring concrete mixer.

The first concrete highway in Indiana stretched from Ft. Wayne to New Haven, Indiana. The highway later became part of the Lincoln Highway.

Brooks Construction Company, Fort Wayne, Indiana collection

ORIGINAL 1915 LINCOLN HIGHWAY ROUTE

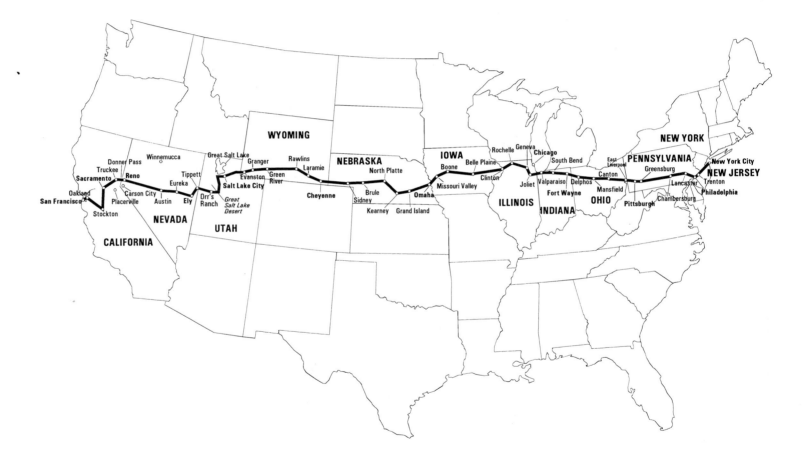

WYOMING

Winnemucca
Donner Pass
Truckee
Sacramento
Oakland
San Francisco
Stockton
Placerville
Carson City
Austin
Eureka
Ely
Tippett
Orr's Ranch
Great Salt Lake Desert
Salt Lake City
Evanston
Green River
Great Salt Lake
Granger
Rawlins
Laramie
Cheyenne
Reno

NEVADA

UTAH

CALIFORNIA

NEBRASKA

North Platte
Brule
Sidney
Kearney
Grand Island
Omaha

IOWA

Boone
Belle Plaine
Missouri Valley
Clinton

Rochelle
Geneva
Chicago
South Bend
Joliet
Valparaiso

ILLINOIS

INDIANA

Fort Wayne

Delphos

OHIO

Mansfield

Canton
East Liverpool
Pittsburgh
Chambersburg

NEW YORK

PENNSYLVANIA

Greensburg

Lancaster

NEW JERSEY

New York City

Trenton
Philadelphia

40 *Link Across America*

ALONG THE LINCOLN HIGHWAY

Cities, Towns, Ranches and Other Reference Points Along the Lincoln Highway

Following is the primary list published by the Lincoln Highway Association in 1916, the places that were added in 1924 because of highway route changes, and the places that were added later.

NEW YORK
New York City

NEW JERSEY
Jersey City
Newark
Elizabeth
Rahway
Iselin
Menlo Park
Metuchen
Highland Park
New Brunswick
Franklin Park
Kingston
Princeton
Lawrenceville
Trenton
1924:   Weehawken

PENNSYLVANIA
Oxford Valley
Glen Lake
Langhorne
La Trippe
Bustleton
No. Philadelphia Station
Philadelphia
Overbrook
Ardmore
Bryn Mawr
Wayne
Berwyn
Paoli
Whitford
Downingtown
Thorndale Station
Coatesville
Sadsburyville
Mt. Vernon
Gap
Kinzers
Leaman Place

Paradise
Soudersburg
Lancaster
Mountville
Columbia
Wrightsville
York
Abbotstown
New Oxford
Gettysburg
Seven Stars
McKnightstown
Cashtown
Grafenberg
Calendonia Park
Fayetteville
West Fayetteville
Chambersburg
St. Thomas
Fort Louden
McConnellsburg
Harrisonville
Breezewood

(continued)

PENNSYLVANIA (continued)

Everett
Mt. Dallas
The Willows
Bedford
Wolfsburg
Schellsburg
Buckstown
Kanter P. 0.
Stoyestown
Jenners
Jennerstown
McLaughlintown
Ligonier
Youngstown
Greensburg
Grapeville
Adamsburg
Irwin
Jacksonville
East McKeesport
Turtle Creek
East Pittsburgh
Wilkinsburg
Pittsburgh
Leetsdale
Fairoaks
Ambridge
Economy

Legionville
Logans
Baden
Conway
Freedom
Rochester
Bridgewater
Beaver
Esther
Ohioville
Smiths Ferry
1924:   Green Tree
          Exton
          Farrilton
          Swickley
1928:   Chester, WV
          Clinton
          Imperial

OHIO

East Liverpool
Lisbon
Hanoverton
Kensington
East Rochester
Minerva
Robertsville
Osnaburg
Canton

Massillon
West Brookfield
East Greenville
Dalton
East Union (Cross Roads)
Wooster
Jefferson
New Pittsburgh
Rowsburg
Ashland
Mansfield
Ontario
Galion
Bucyrus
Nevada
Upper Sandusky
Forest
Dunkirk
Dola
Ada
Lima
Gomer
Delphos
Van Wert
1924:   Crestline
          Leesville
          Oceola
          Williamstown
          New Stark
          Beaverdam   *(continued)*

Cities, Towns, Ranches and Other Reference Points Along the Lincoln Highway (continued)

OHIO (continued)
    Cairo
1928:   Jeromesville
    Hayesville
    Mifflin

INDIANA
New Haven
Fort Wayne
Cherubusco
Merriam
Wolf Lake
Kimmell
Ligonier
Benton
Goshen
Elkhart
Osceola
Mishawaka
South Bend
New Carlisle
La Porte
Westville
Valparaiso
Deep River
Merrillville
Schererville
Dyer
1928:   Wanatah

Hanna
Hamlet
Groverstown
Donaldson
Plymouth
Inwood
Bourbon
Etna Green
Atwood
Warsaw
Columbia City

ILLINOIS
Chicago Heights
Joliet
Plainfield
Aurora
Mooseheart
Batavia
Geneva
De Kalb
Malta
Creston
Rochelle
Ashton
Franklin Grove
Nachusa
Dixon
Sterling

Morrison
Fulton
1924:   New Lennox

IOWA
Clinton
Elvira
De Witt
Grand Mound
Calamus
Wheatland
Lowden
Clarence
Stanwood
Mechanicsville
Lisbon
Mt. Vernon
Marion
Cedar Rapids
Belle Plain
Chelsea
Gladstone
Tama
Montour
Butlerville
Le Grand
Marshalltown
La Moille

(continued)

Cities, Towns, Ranches and Other Reference Points Along the Lincoln Highway (continued)

IOWA (continued)
Colo
Nevada
Ames
Ontario
Jordan
Boone
Ogden
Grand Junction
Jefferson
Scranton
Ralston
Glidden
Carroll
Westside
Vail
Denison
Arion
Dow City
Dunlap
Woodbine
Logan
Missouri Valley
Loveland
Honey Creek
Crescent
Council Bluffs
1924:   State Center

NEBRASKA
Omaha
Elkhorn
Waterloo
Valley
Fremont
Ames
North Bend
Rogers
Schuyler
Benton Station or Richland P.O.
Columbus
Duncan
Silver Creek
Clarks
Central City
Chapman
Grand Island
Alda
Wood River
Shelton
Gibbon
Kearney
Odessa
Elm Creek
Overton
Lexington
Cozad
Gothenburg

Brady Island
Maxwell
North Platte
Hershey
Sutherland
Paxton
Roscoe
Ogallala
Brule
Megeath (R.R. Flag Station)
Big Springs
Chappell
Lodge Pole
Sunol
Sidney
Potter
Dix Station
Kimball
Bushnell
1924:   Haven
            Josselyn
            Willow Island
            Brownson
1928:   Blair

WYOMING
Pinebluffs
Egbert

(continued)

Cities, Towns, Ranches and Other Reference Points Along the Lincoln Highway (continued)

WYOMING (continued)
Burns
Archer
Cheyenne
Corlett Station
Borie Station
Otto Station
Granite Canyon Station
Buford Station
Sherman Hill
Laramie
Bosler
Cooper Lake
Lookout Station
Harper (Section House)
Rock River
Medicine Bow
Allen Station
Hanna
Fort Steele
Lakota (Section House)
Granville (Pumping House)
Rawlins
Creston Station
Latham Station
Wamsutter
Point of Rocks
Thayer Junction
Rock Springs

Green River
Bryan Station
Granger
Lyman
Fort Bridger
Evanston
1924:   Carbon
         Parco (Sinclair)
         Red Desert
         Tipton Station

UTAH
Wyuta Station
Wasatch
Castle Rock
Emory Station
Main Forks
Coalville
Hoytsville
Wanship
Kimball's Ranch
Roach's Ranch
Salt Lake City
East Garfield (or Pleasant Green)
Ragtown (Italian Minor Settlement)
Garfield
Lakepoint
Milltown

Grantsville
Timpie Point
Iosepa (Kanaka Ranch)
Brown's Ranch
Indian Ranch
Indian Farm or Severe Ranch
Orr's Ranch
County Well
Fish Springs (J. J. Thomas Ranch)
Callao (Kearney's Ranch)
Ibapah
1924:   Magna
         Tooele
         Stockton
         St. John
         Bush Ranch
         Willow Springs Ranch
         Fisher Pass (Johnson Pass)
         Granite Mountain
         Black Point
         Gold Hill

NEVADA
Tippett Ranch
Anderson's Ranch
Schellbourne (Burke's Ranch)
Magnuson Ranch
McGill

(continued)

NEVADA (continued)
East Ely
Ely
Lane City
Copper Flat
Riepetown
Kimberly
Jakes Summit
Mooreman's Ranch
Rosevear's Ranch
White Pine Summit
Six Mile House
Pancake Summit
Fourteen Mile House
Pinto House
Eureka
Austin
New Pass
Alpine (Shoshone Indian Ranch)
Eastgate
Westgate
Frenchman's Station
Sand Springs
Salt Wells
Grimes Ranch
Fallon
Hazen
Fernly
Wadsworth

Derby
Vista Station
Sparks
Reno (There were two alternative Lincoln Highway routes from Reno to Sacramento)
#1:   Verdi, NV

CALIFORNIA
Truckee
Donner Lake
Emigrant Gap
Alta
Gold Run
Colfax
Wymar
Applegate
Auburn
Newcastle
Penryn
Loomis
Rocklin
Roseville
Sacramento

#2:   **NEVADA**
Reno
Steamboat Springs
Washoe
Franktown
Carson City
Glenbrook
Cave Rock
#3   1924:   Leeteville
                 Dayton, NV

CALIFORNIA
Edgewood
Lakeside Park
Myers
Sierra Nevada Summit
Phillips
Strawberry
Kyburz
Riverton
Sportmans Hall
Camino
Placerville
Eldorado

(continued)

Cities, Towns, Ranches and Other Reference Points Along the Lincoln Highway (continued)

CALIFORNIA (continued)
- Shingle Springs
- Clarksville
- White Rock
- Folsom
- Natoma
- Mills
- Mayhew
- Manlove
- Perkins
- Sacramento

(From Sacramento to San Francisco)

- Elk Grove
- McConnell
- Arno
- Galt
- Woodbridge
- Stockton
- French Camp
- Banta
- Tracy
- Altamont

- Livermore
- Hayward
- Oakland
- San Francisco
- 1924: Lodi, CA
- 1928: Davis
- Dixon
- Vacaville
- Fairfield
- Vallejo
- San Pablo

For more information about the Lincoln Highway, contact The Lincoln Highway Association, P.O. Box 308, Franklin Grove, Illinois 61031.

BIBLIOGRAPHY

Hokanson, Drake, *The Lincoln Highway: Main Street Across America,* University of Iowa Press, Iowa City, Iowa, 1988

The Complete Official Road Guide of The Lincoln Highway, The Lincoln Highway Association, 1924; Patrice Press, Tucson, Arizona, 1993

The Lincoln Highway Forum, The Lincoln Highway Association, Vol. 1, No. 2—Winter 1993

Mary Elizabeth Anderson has published articles in more than 60 regional and national publications. This is her first published children's book. She grew up in Shenandoah, Iowa, graduated from Northwest Missouri State University with a Bachelor of Science in Education degree, and has taught students from kindergarten through eighth grade. Currently, in addition to pursuing her writing career, she teaches adult creative writing classes throughout Iowa and Nebraska. Mary Elizabeth Anderson lives in Grand Island, Nebraska with her husband, Don.

About Rayve Productions

Rayve Productions is an award-winning small publisher of books and music. Current publications are mainly in the following categories:

(1) Business guidebooks for home-based businesses and other entrepreneurs

(2) Quality children's books and music

(3) History books about America and her regions, and an heirloom-quality journal for creating personal histories.

Rayve Productions' mail-order catalog offers the above items plus business books, software, music, and other enjoyable items produced by others.

Our eclectic collection of business resources and gift items has something to please everyone.

A FREE catalog is available upon request.

CHILDREN'S BOOKS & MUSIC FROM RAYVE PRODUCTIONS

The Perfect Orange, A tale from Ethiopia

by Frank P. Araujo, PhD; illustrated by Xiao Jun Li

ISBN 1-877810-94-0, hardcover, $16.95, 1994 pub., Toucan Tales volume 2

Inspiring gentle folktale. Breathtaking watercolors dramatize ancient Ethiopia's contrasting pastoral charm, majesty. Illustrations are rich with Ethiopian details. Story reinforces values of generosity and selflessness over greed and self-centeredness.

(PBS *Storytime* Selection. Recommended by *School Library Journal, Faces, MultiCultural Review, Small Press Magazine, The Five Owls, Wilson Library Bulletin*)

THE PERFECT ORANGE

A Tale from Ethiopia

Frank P. Araujo, PhD
Illustrations by Xiao Jun Li

Nekane, the Lamiña & the Bear, A tale of the Basque Pyrenees

by Frank P. Araujo, PhD; illustrated by Xiao Jun Li

ISBN 1-877810-01-0, hardcover, $16.95, 1993 pub., Toucan Tales volume 1

Delightful Basque folktale pits appealing, quick-witted young heroine against mysterious villain. Lively, imaginative narrative, sprinkled with Basque phrases. Vibrant watercolor images. Glossary of Basque terms and pronunciation key.

(Recommended by *School Library Journal, Publishers Weekly, Kirkus Reviews, Booklist, Wilson Library Bulletin, Basque Studies Program Newsletter: University of Nevada, BCCB, The Five Owls*)

The Laughing River, A folktale for peace

by Elizabeth Haze Vega; illustrated by Ashley Smith, 1995 pub.

ISBN 1-877810-35-5, hardcover book, $16.95

ISBN 1-877810-36-3, companion musical audiotape, $9.95

ISBN 1-877810-37-1, book & musical audiotape combo, $23.95

Drum Kit, $9.95

Individual Set: 1 book + 1 musical audiotape + kit for making 1 drum, $29.95

Group Set: 1 book + 1 musical audiotape + kit for making 6 drums + teachers guide, $59.95

Class Set: 1 book + 1 musical audiotape + kit for making 30 drums + teachers guide, $199.95

Teachers guide for students of all ages, $4.95

Two fanciful African tribes are in conflict until the laughing river bubbles melodiously into their lives, bringing fun, friendship, peace. Lyrical fanciful folktale of conflict resolution. Mesmerizing music. Dancing, singing and drumming instructions. Orff approach.

(Recommended by *School Library Journal*)

(*continued on following page*)

CHILDREN'S BOOKS & MUSIC FROM RAYVE PRODUCTIONS

(continued from previous page)

When Molly Was in the Hospital
A book for brothers and sisters of hospitalized children

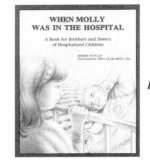

by Debbie Duncan; illustrated by Nina Ollikainen, MD
ISBN 1-877810-44-4, hardcover, $12.95, 1994 pub.
Sensitive, insightful, supportive story for all who care about ill children . . . and their families.
Authentic. Realistic. Effective.
(Recommended by *Children's Book Insider, School Library Journal,
Disabilities Resources Monthly*)

*Winner of 1995
Benjamin Franklin Award
Best Children's Picture Book*

Night Sounds by Lois G. Grambling; illustrated by Randall F. Ray, 1996 pub.
ISBN 1-877810-77-0, hardcover, $12.95
ISBN 1-877810-83-5, softcover, $6.95
Perfect bedtime story. Ever so gently, a child's thoughts slip farther and farther away, moving from purring cat at bedside and comical creatures in the yard to distant trains and church bells, and then at last, to sleep. Imaginative, lilting text and daringly unpretentious b/w watercolor illustrations

Los Sonidos de la Noche by Lois G. Grambling; illustrated by Randall F. Ray
(Spanish edition of *Night Sounds*), 1996 pub.
ISBN 1-877810-76-2, hardcover, $12.95
ISBN 1-877810-82-7, softcover, $6.95

Link Across America, A story of the historic Lincoln Highway by Mary Elizabeth Anderson
ISBN 1-877810-97-5, hardcover, $14.95, 1997 pub.

ORDER TOLL-FREE 24 HOURS A DAY, ANY DAY **800.852.4890**
FREE catalog available on request
Come visit us at *www.spannet.org/rayve/*
Rayve Productions Box 726 Windsor CA 95492 • 707.838.6200 • rayvepro@aol.com • fax 707.838.2220